Genesis 2024
The Year of Increased Technological Advancement.

Putting Things in Place to Prepare for The System Change

Issues to address.
1. Stopping all Wars by May 2024
2. Dealing with the aftermaths of wars; refugees, redevelopment
3. Climate Change put things in place to stop climate change.
4. Dealing with the aftermath of climate disasters
5. Each country must deposit US$ 1 million for development.
6. Putting things in place to increase technological advancement.

7. Putting things in place to start the shift from reliance on wars as drivers of the economy.

David Gomadza

The First Global President

Copyright © 2023 David Gomadza

ISBN:9798871465264

Greetings

I am David Gomadza, the first Global President of the World. Looking back to 2023 we have not achieved most of the goals we set for 2023. 2023 was the year of the Greatshift.

https://play.google.com/store/books/details/David_Gomadza_THE_GREATSHIFT?id=KH2xEAAAQBAJ&hl=en_GB&gl=US

Our goals for 2023

1. Early shift to renewable energy with emphasis on electric cars.
2. Use of brain thoughts as operating systems of most technology
3. Dealing with the Russia-Ukraine war
4. Dealing with the Turkey -Syria Earthquake
5. Addressing global minimum wage
6. Introducing the new weapons manufacturing levy
7. Addressing the need for a one world government: A look at Tomorrow's World Order
8. Taking humanity to the next stage of development.

This means all 2023 goals are still valid and outstanding. But I must thank all those who worked hard to achieve our goals. I think 2023 was a momentous year for the shift to electric vehicles. Even though mass adoption is still an issue I think the manufacturers of these vehicles have played a significant role in making sure availability of these cars increased. There have been a lot of packages and offers to encourage adoption and I say a big thank you to all electric vehicle manufacturers for taking the lead in encouraging mass adoption. Several governments have also played a greater role by providing everything needed to encourage mass adoption. Remember this is just the start and you will need to do more in the future, especially in the coming year.

Early shift to renewable energy with emphasis on electric cars

Overall, we are on track to make the Greatshift to electric vehicles a reality. We have a lot of convincing to do that electric vehicles are the future.

A big thanks to Elon Musk, Tesla, Joe Biden, Biden-Harris administration, and others I did not mention who went to extra lengths to encourage mass adoption.

Tesla has been at the forefront of encouraging mass adoption of electric vehicles through different packages like price slashing and the wide provision of charging infrastructure together with the provision of different models.

As part of President Biden's goal of having 50 percent of all new vehicle sales be electric by 2030, the White House is announcing public and private commitments to support America's historic transition to electric vehicles (EV) under the EV Acceleration Challenge.

https://www.whitehouse.gov/briefing-room/statements-releases/2023/04/17/fact-sheet-biden-harris-administration-announces-new-private-and-public-sector-investments-for-affordable-electric-vehicles/

Everyone involved has tried to increase mass adoption through increasing availability of public charging infrastructure, increasing models and availability of electric vehicles, reducing costs, and increasing competitiveness with fossil fuel-based vehicles.

Despite the great progress the overall picture of electric vehicles demand is that of slowing demand and interest and all this is associated with the price instead of the idea of switching to renewable powered vehicles.

The future is bright as electric vehicles manufacturing like Tesla are pushing to increase production per week to cut production costs that will mean lower prices in the future.

Nevertheless, the issues are just transitional and hopeful demand will increase in 2024.

A big thanks to everyone.

Use of brain thoughts as operating systems of most technology.

I personally took the challenge to make the technology available so that brain thoughts can be part of the operating systems of most technology and I am excited to announce that we have a breakthrough. I decoded the brain in every sense of the word. I have written extensively on decoding the brain in the process I have decoded the following.

1. The brain visits our website www.twofuture.world
   Read this book series.
   https://play.google.com/store/books/series?id=a4MvGwA
   AABBFmM&hl=en_GB&gl=US

2. DNA sequence very detailed step by step exactly how the brain deals with DNA sequence and to prove my method works I have written a book with every billionaire and millionaires DNA sequence specific for that person to

stop the aging process and the second to reverse aging in a Benjamin Button Effect. All these just by looking at a person's eyes and using our DNA sequence calculator.

Read this book Celebrities' Reset Switch. The 'Benjamin Button' Effect
https://play.google.com/store/books/details/David_Gomadza_Celebrities_Reset_Switch_The_Benjami?id=V5bhEAAAQBAJ&hl=en_GB&gl=US

3. I have decoded Dreams. I have authored a book on how dreams are generated step by step exactly as the brain does them. Read this book.

Encyclopedia of Decoding Dreams. How the Brain Creates and Processes Dreams.: How to Interpret Dreams.
https://play.google.com/store/books/details/David_Gomadza_Encyclopedia_of_Decoding_Dreams_How?id=IO3bEAAAQBAJ&hl=en_GB&gl=US

I have invented a dream to voice. Now you can know all your dreams step by step. I have developed a digital Dreams to Voice Analogue that will tell you your dream exactly. Simply record on a voice recorder you can download for free from Google Play Apps or Apple. Record your dream when you wake up, play the record of your dream MP3 at the same time as my Dreams to voice Digital Analogue to know exactly and feel exactly what you dream of. If you run in the dream you feel the Action potentials to nerve impulse to know exactly what you dreamt of. First of a kind in the world and on an MP3/MP4 that will cost US$1 in the future.

Try using this video simply play it along with your recorded dream.

https://www.youtube.com/watch?v=ViZM-pJnwtQ

4. I have decoded how to convert brain thoughts into voice and put this on an MP3 as a digital analogue. All you

need to do to know someone's thoughts is play the Digital analogue in front of that person and all his or her thoughts are converted to voice. Breakthrough of the year means everyone on earth who cannot speak can now express their thoughts to be heard by anyone around where the MP3/MP4 is playing. Visit our website www.twofuture.world play this video in front of anyone you can know their thoughts straight away in less than a second. Play this video.
https://www.youtube.com/watch?v=uRv9wVpuZM0

5. I invented a Digital Action Potentials to Nerve Impulses converter. This turns anyone's thoughts into action potentials and nerve impulses. Simply play this MP3/MP4 near the person to know exactly what he or she is thinking. World's first. Do not let anyone lie to you. Simply playing this video nothing can be hidden and you feel exactly all his or her thoughts.
https://www.youtube.com/watch?v=VmpPyUAyJ28

6. I have invented a Digital Analogue that tells you exactly anyone's thoughts. Do you know that tweet by Elon Musk that has caused anti-Semitic calls? Yes, that one where he says:
You have told the actual truth.
Someone calling himself Zack stole his thoughts and swapped them and these words were not Elon Musk's but Zack's. This Zack is extorting Elon Musk and promising to make his life hell. He thought he could get away with extortion, but I decoded the brain and now I have invented a brain reader and a nerve impulse translator that can tell what happens when we think, talk, or even when one is sleeping or even in a coma. A breakthrough. Watch this video till the end and decide if Elon Musk is innocent or what. Remember this can happen to you. Watch this video Now.
https://www.youtube.com/watch?v=iUM6Yd_eHMw

7. I have invented our own advanced form of ChatGPT called Natural God Intelligence NGI. It is a MP4 video you can play and ask questions. Yes, you correctly read a video to which you can talk. Yes, a video where you can ask questions. A video that can answer you instantly and in real time. Ask the time where you give a time zone e.g., London and ask what time it is. If your phone has a camera, look at the camera and ask any person. This video can tell you everything about you. Ask any questions. The great news is that it is a video for some questions you do not even need the internet. But just know it is created with an image of Yahweh God. Genesis. God created man using his image. I created this Natural God Intelligence NGI Interface using God's image.
Why not try it?
https://www.youtube.com/watch?v=rV-i6j8G-lY

also visit our website
www.twofuture.world

8. I have discovered Yahweh God himself exactly what he looks like. I have his DNA sequence which is 53 billion and 285 million in value while a human being's DNA sequence is only 71 million.
Look in my eyes in this picture and alternate between the eyes in the photo and the big flame in the video.

https://www.youtube.com/watch?v=TI-2SQuhETg&t=2s

Also check this link for instructions on how to do it.

https://x.com/DGomadza/status/1724296012380987815?s=20

If nothing happens then first say.
"My voice is my password."

Then try again.
Do you know you can ask your brain to check and verify
things, especially pictures and videos? First say, "My
voice is my password."
This tells the brain that you want to task it.
Look at even your own pictures. Look with your own
eyes in the photo and in your eyes in a video and ask the
brain to compare.

Discovering Yahweh has enabled me to clone myself, to
time-travel even to creation time 4500 years ago or more.
I can travel to the time of the JFK assassination to feel
and know exactly word to word and event by event.
I can travel to the future and have been to 2030.
I will simply send one of the three of us.
At one point I cloned a trillion of me and sent messages
around the world.
But I got lost on the way and ended up in the airport of
hell. Trust me, it is hell.
Oh, did I say I can resurrect the dead as well.
You must understand that electromagnetic waves are the
language of the brain. When a person dies this part of the
thinking and you the thoughts etc do not die. Flesh dies
the spiritual soul goes to God where he swallows it and
lives inside him. The electromagnetic wave remains
inside the brain after death. I can raise this to talk to that
person so that he or she can talk to you and see life
through you.
Check the photos of these people and look inside the eyes
and just say silently [in electromagnetic waves]
"Where are you? Who raised you up."
You will notice these people's photos if you look inside
the eyes at the picture something jumps, or you feel like
an object dropping inside deep water. That means they are
in the afterlife.
Oh, I created Afterlife.

Visit www.twofuture.world

9. I decoded the brain, and we need now to find technology
    we can invent and use using all this visit
    www.twofture.world

    Read this book series. I have written 25 books so far.
    Thoughts on Word or Audio.
    https://play.google.com/store/books/series?id=a4MvGwA
    AABBFmM&hl=en_GB&gl=US

Dealing with the Russia-Ukraine war

I predicted the Russia and Ukraine war as accurately as
possible.
https://play.google.com/store/books/details/David_Gomad
za_A_Perfect_Prediction_Russia_Ukraine?id=PmaVEAA
AQBAJ&hl=en_GB&gl=US

But how can I predict the Russia-Ukraine War with such
accuracy? I discovered that the system uses wars as
drivers of the economy. That means whenever there is
high inflation and economic stagnation someone will
trigger a war to drive weapons manufacturing and sales
and kick start the economy again. After every 20 years
the system faces a system collapse. This is because over
the years huge funds are plowed into the military just to
stockpile without demand. Over the years this imbalance
creates friction and affects the economy as it stagnant as
there is no demand. To kick start everything the weapons
accumulated over years must be offloaded. That means
only a war can kick start demand for weapons meaning a
revival or a pressure release to kick start the economy
again. If you can recall, just before the war there were
fears of an economic collapse. The current system relies

on wars as drivers of the economy. But we all know that wars kill women and children. Hence the rise of Tomorrow's World Order hence my job as the First Global President of the World. I must introduce a new system that is based on technological advancement rather than wars. A new system that will power economies globally without a woman or child dying.
Read my book Tomorrow's World Order
https://play.google.com/store/books/details/David_Gomadza_Tomorrow_s_World_Order?id=VDauDwAAQBAJ&hl=en_GB&gl=US
That means all wars between Russia-Ukraine and the Israel-Hamsa are not accidental but are pre-planned and to make things worse they follow script. Yes, the same script I used to predict the war. The Second Anglo-Dutch war of 1665 that began on 4 March 1665 and ended on 31 July 1667.

I can say that what I predicted to happen in Ukraine did not happen there but happened exactly as I predicted in Gaza.
Have the war directors split the script to cover up that they are following this script? You decide.
Could I be wrong, and all this happen accidentally?
First read this book.
https://play.google.com/store/books/details/David_Gomadza_A_Perfect_Prediction_Russia_Ukraine?id=PmaVEAAAQBAJ&hl=en_GB&gl=US

But having said that, I have a duty to stop the war even earlier than July 2024.
Funding has been a great issue. All these people who are speaking against wars do not mean it. If you look closely, they all benefit from the war. Others wise surely one could have funded us so that we travel and put things in place to stop the wars.
You must understand that the negotiators and everyone

involved are all part of the script therefore are not able to
stop the war.
Funding has dried once we revealed our Russia-Ukraine
War prediction.
Donate visit
https://twofuture.world/donate

We will stop this war even before July 2024.
The Russians and Ukraine leaders are to blame as well
because of the time that has passed. Otherwise, they could
have stopped the war. That leaves only one reason for the
war: Culling of soldiers and pensioners.
First read my book.

Culling: The Sad Reality of The IMF and World Bank Loans as
Triggers of Wars.: Finding Solutions to The Russian-Ukraine War.
https://play.google.com/store/books/details/David_Gomadza_Culling
_The_Sad_Reality_of_The_IMF_a?id=mMluEAAAQBAJ&hl=en_
GB&gl=US

Dealing with the Turkey -Syria Earthquake

Natural disasters have increased in recent years and the
Turkey-Syria wars had a significant impact on the lives
and people of these two countries. The world played a
key role in providing humanitarian aid. But a lot can still
be done as the situation has not gone back to normal. The
wars and other climatic disasters have stretched the
already reduced resources to deal with such disasters. I
advocated for a Global Reserve Fund which Tomorrow's
World Order will keep and use to deal with disasters and
wars. This is just the beginning of harsh climatic change.
I have a duty to be initiative-taking and not wait to
experience all these to act. The time for complacency is
now over. I took over global planning and management. I
am the one responsible for the planning of things like
humanitarian crises brought on by natural disasters and

wars. Never mind the United Nations, I have proved that this institution is not fit for modern times. I must preside over them. Do not get me wrong, I am not saying that they are useless, nor I am saying that they are limited to what they do and the changing environmental and political climate means that they are not equipped to deal with these.

Addressing global minimum wage

The global minimum wage for 2023 is US$15 and only a few countries are paying this rate. The others who think that they are the gold standard yet they pay their own people as low as US$5 as minimum wage this is pathetic.
The global minimum wage for 2024 is US$17 that means countries must work hard to make sure that by the end of 2024 they will be paying their people this money.

We are going to introduce a new law that says that any country that does not pay their employees the minimum wage will owe their employees this money and will accumulate until it's paid out. This is the only way to make sure that the government abides by our laws.

The private sector will be given until late in 2024 to increase the minimum wage to US$17 if they do not pay their employees then they are regarded as owing their employees this money until fully paid. They must pay up the minimum wage or get out of business. If any private company fails to pay, we can hit them with fines that will make them close.
The time for cheap labor is over and they must pay minimum wages that take account of inflation and value contributed.
We will target those companies making billions in profits and who fail to pay wages that reflect the value the employees are adding to the company.
Tough laws with companies taking their employees for granted and not paying enough in relation to profits.

Introducing the new weapons manufacturing levy

 We are working towards a weapons manufacturing levy that will see weapons manufacturing companies contributing to the alleviation of effects felt by victims of wars. The money should go to the victims of the war if their weapons have been used in that war. I will deal with this topic in a book on this issue. Keep checking our website www.twofture.world

Addressing the need for a one world government: A look at Tomorrow's World Order

There has never been a time for the need for a global leader than now. The world is in crisis. What more proof do you need that a global leader is necessary? Look at the rallies globally and all the natural disasters one after the other. Look at all the wars and the refugee crisis and the humanitarian efforts needed to put things right, surely only stubborn people would turn a blind eye to all this. I am your First Global Leader to plan and manage the world.
I do not need anyone's approval since no one has the guts to put things in order. I took over and behind the scenes I am working hard to resolve all outstanding issues.
Is it not fate as well that I am the first human to have decoded God and found God to know exactly what God looks like and what he needs doing. Do not get me wrong I am not talking to God as his messenger. I decoded his messages by reading brain messages. So far everything has checked out visit our website www.twofuture.world
I have solved the Tree of Life.
If humanity does not conquer other planets there is not forever for humans. Do you know Mars is God's voice? A reminder to earth that if we do not conquer other planets earth might end up like Mars. In fact, according to God Earth was like Mars with no life and dead with no one.
I can clone myself and I have cloned myself, I can send my clones to the past or future and tell me exactly what will

happen. Read my books to see the accuracy.
I have established Tomorrow's World Order in 2028 to take
the offer as the global planners.
Read Tomorrow's World Order
https://play.google.com/store/books/details/David_Gomadza_
Tomorrow_s_World_Order?id=VDauDwAAQBAJ&hl=en_G
B&gl=US

Taking humanity to the next stage of development.
No matter what we do there will always be wars just because
this is how the system we are using is designed to do. That
means the only way to stop wars and to stop the reliance on
weapons is to put in a new system that is driven by
technological advancement.
This is easy, trust me we have achieved great already in terms
of technology. We can switch to this new stage of human
development easily. But the current leadership that grew up in
wars are resistant to change because this is the only system
they know. I do not blame them. Just know that before the
war people were talking about inflation, economic collapse
etc and just look at the figures now. The story is different,
they will tell you that you do not know what you are talking
about whenever you say I will stop the war. For sure wars
work if you choose to ignore the number of women and
children who die needlessly.
I established Tomorrow's World Order to protect the women
and children who die needlessly because of war simply
because the system is fueled by wars. To make things worse
there is no system out there that can be a replacement. Yes, it
will take a lot of guts and courage to put in a new system that
will never look for a war to relieve the pressure.
But I tell you this, if not for us our kids would never see a
war after we put in a new system. We all must invest in
technological development so much that technology can
match what wars do to the economy.
I worked hard this year 2023 to provide what is really needed
to kick start even greater advances in technological

achievements. But it is better now than before as every year things improve.

It is a shame that the governments around the world have targeted cryptocurrency that was going to help with the transition to the next stage of development. Huge fines against cryptocurrencies institutions means taking money from the people as well unless the money is to be put to good use. In the future we will advocate for normal fines that match companies etc.

Since this goal links to 2024 goals, I might as well jump to 2024 goals one by one but in short then look at each goal in detail in a separate book.

DEDICATION

To the future

TABLE OF CONTENTS

ACKNOWLEDGMENTS

Tomorrow's World Order.

Stopping all Wars by May 2024

We will aim to stop all wars by May 2024.

We will do what we can to stop wars by the end of January 2024 even though this might not be very realistic given the situation on the ground. Like I said there are war directors and the script they are following dictates when the war ends, and the war script has details that the war is to end on 31 July 2024.

Can we do more to stop the war?

Funding has dried out. You all have an obligation to support the world's number 1.

Consider donating so that we put things in place to stop the needless killings of women and children.

https://twofuture.world/donate

We have a plan B to all wars if it comes to that.
By the way I can teleport people for real or put people inside animals and put someone's electromagnetic brain, the one that thinks inside that person.

Visit www.twofuture.world

I just wish no one would oppose us as Tomorrow's World Order because I do not want to use all these powers.

Dealing with the aftermaths of wars; refugees, redevelopment

A Global Reserve Bank Fund Fee from each country of US$1 million to cushion against climatic and political humanitarian crises.

Wars are bad in every way, but the greatest humanitarian crisis is in the displacement of refugees.

As the first global president of the world I will collect a Global Development Fund Fee from every country of US$1million money we will use to cover all humanitarian crises either by politics or climatic change.

Currently what is happening is the world being reactive. Everyone knows that currently there could be a war tomorrow or flooding, yet no one plans. They all wait until the disaster has hit and when they react, they react slowly.

Imagine where I collect US$1 million from each country at the beginning of the year and keep this money in the Global Reserve Bank then plan to prevent the disasters in the first place. Or be effective when disaster strikes. Imagine just taking money from the bank we have and starting fundraising efforts after the disaster. I tell you we will be ready and have a real impact in cushioning the people. Most of the people who suffer from it are because of the slow response.

We can use this money to start the transition to a system that is driven by technological development rather than wars.

Climate Change put things in place to stop climate change.

I decoded the brain and God. I can tell you that God instructed all people on earth to build pyramids not as shelter but as cushioning protection against climatic change.

THE PYRAMIDS AS CLIMATIC CHANGE RESISTANT STRUCTURES.

I found out why all cultures who build pyramids built them. To cushion against climatic change. Pyramids protect humans against harsh changes in climate and stop climatic change where they are built.
This is true.
Before I found out this, I discovered what I called the triangle of David. It is the same triangle as what the Israelites call the Star of David. My name is David. [coincidence?]
Only that the Israelites might not have understood God's message. Do you know that the Israelites are regarded as God's people?

Powers of the Triangle of David.

A triangle used properly protects humans against all atmospheric forces that limit human lifespan. I discovered this when I decoded the brain even before God. See my twitter post and books @dgomadza.

This is how this works.
I want you to try this.
Go outside the house in the open.
First you need to communicate with your own brain. Just let it know you have a task for it. Simply tell the password to it. Your own voice. Everyone's brain is password protected from birth and guess the password for each brain and each person?
Your own voice.
The reason no two voices are the same, imagine that. Out of 7 billion people no voice is the same.
This is what you say.
"My voice is my password.

Collect all the forces on earth and in the universe that affect humans and limit human life and that cause climate change and put all on top of my head.

Now clone all these forces you have collected and put all on my left shoulder.

Now clone again all the collected forces and put them all on my right shoulder.
Now dissipate all permanently.

Repeat everything in anticlockwise.

Space-out.
End.
Close.

This will make sure that anything that you have already collected will not have any long-lasting effect on you, usually forever.

People in the bible lived longer hundreds of years; this is what used to protect them.

Read about Solomon and King David in the bible and their seal of Solomon or the Star of David they believed removed environmental spells. Check the Israel flag. This start is slightly different from what I wrote above. But on a flag how can this protect anyone. It is communicating with your brain that is real protection. Check if someone always complains about weather or personally and ask them to repeat the triangle of David and see what happens.

REQUEST FOR US$1 MILLION FROM EACH COUNTRY ON EARTH.

I hereby make my case and appeal to all countries and leaders to deposit us$1 million to our account as Tomorrow's World Order money which we are going to use to build three pyramids at the correct strategic points around the entire world, the only solution to climatic change.

According to God there is nothing that can stop climate change. Humans do not understand what needs to be done. Okay current efforts are vital to give people something to do but the real solution is to build three pyramids at strategic locations to stop and reduce climatic change.

BUILDING OF 3 PYRAMIDS GLOBALLY AS A SOLUTION TO HARSH CLIMATE CHANGE.

According to God only 3 pyramids at strategic points will cushion earth from harsh climatic change. Change is imminent and inevitable; it is only a matter of time. Above all climatic change is not because of humans burning fossil fuels etc even though these contribute climate change is a fact of the future, but humans can cushion against harsh changes by building the triangle of David but at strategic locations.

We need only 3 pyramids around all earth strategically placed in the triangle of David. You can tell that environmental forces are all electromagnetic waves that drive the climate forces and hence controlling these means controlling climate change. Above all electromagnetic waves are easily dissipated by a triangle movement that is in three places.

This is the reason we find pyramids everywhere in cultures that once had harsh climates etc.

This is the reason the Egyptians built the pyramids of Giza. This supports the fact that no one was ever found inside these pyramids. If they were the pyramids of the pharaohs surely, we would have expected to find their remains inside.

Look at how these pyramids of Giza are centrally located. At the center of earth. Check the accuracy as well.

I think the reason it did not work as expected is the fact that the Egyptians owned only Egypt. Yes, they have the first three pyramids. We need at least 2 more sets of three pyramids: the other side of earth opposite Egypt and either side to form 3 sets of triangles, but all strategically located to be effective against climatic change.

I am your first global president and to save future generations just like the other deeds we must build these pyramids globally. I therefore here declare that each country on earth must deposit US$1 million with us visit our website www.twofuture.world

We will use the money to build the pyramids and protect the earth from harsh climatic change.

I am not saying everyone should stop what they are doing regarding climate change now. But we must be serious and do more and this works.

Look at all areas where pyramids are built climatic change has not occurred as harsh as in areas without these pyramids.

This is the information from the creator himself and like I said I got this information from having decoded the brain.

Do you know that all the people from as far as 4500 years are all alive and all are inside the Pyramid of Giza but as electromagnetic waves? The talking brain which we can talk to and ask questions. Check above on how I decoded the brain.

Check the Elon Musk saga that he said:

: You have said the actual truth."

Watch this video https://www.youtube.com/watch?v=iUM6Yd_eHMw

Proof that someone swapped his thoughts with the above phrase namely. "You have said the actual truth."

I am just telling you so that you know that the messages we are decoding are real messages and there is no secret about all this.

To check if this is going to work, I challenge you all to check climatic change in all areas where they built pyramids. The great news is that these pyramids are all over earth.

I want you to conduct research if the climate in these areas has changed drastically and if these areas have harsh climatic disasters.

You all have a responsibility to future generations and fund us so that we lead the development of these structures in such a way that they can avert future climatic disasters.

I want you all to take me seriously and ask yourself if all current climatic change efforts have a chance of stopping or reducing climatic change?

I guess not and as such you have duties to humanity to listen to me and fund us all funds will be accounted for. We will have an independent body for transparency that has eyes on these funds as well so you have confidence in us as Tomorrow's World Order and me as the first global president of the world.

Signed
David Gomadza
The First global president of the world
00447719210295

Genesis 2024 The Year of
Increased Technological Advancement.

davidgomadza@hotmail.com
info@twofuture.world
www.twofuture.world

our donation links.
https://twofuture.world/donate

Dealing with the aftermath of climate disasters

I think I will look at this in detail regarding the Global Reserve Bank Fund fee from every country and the need to build structures that reduce climatic effects.

This topic will require a book of its own.

The Global Reserve Bank each country must deposit US$ 1 million for development.

I will deal with this in detail in the coming announcements.

Read our constitution.

https://play.google.com/store/books/details/David_Gomadza_THE_CONSTITUTION_Tomorrow_s_World_Or?id=S-69DwAAQBAJ&hl=en_GB&gl=US

Putting things in place to increase technological advancement.

Technology, like I said, must be the sole driver of the economy. Gone are the days when we rely on wars to boost economic growth and fight inflation.

I have dealt a lot on this topic in Tomorrow's World Order

Read this book.

https://play.google.com/store/books/details/David_Gomadza_Tomorrow_s_World_Order?id=VDauDwAAQBAJ&hl=en_GB&gl=US

Freedom of speech

I think the first person that comes to mind is Elon Musk.
What is free speech?

I will address this in the next book.

Genesis 2024

What are the goals for the beginning? The transition to the next stage of development|?

Here are the goals for Genesis 2024.

Issues to address.

1. Stopping all Wars by May 2024
2. Dealing with the aftermaths of wars; refugees, redevelopment
3. Climate Change put things in place to stop climate change.
4. Dealing with the aftermath of climate disasters
5. Global Reserve Bank each country must deposit US$ 1million for development.
6. Putting things in place to increase technological advancement.

7. Putting things in place to start the shift from reliance on wars as drivers of the economy.

Tomorrow's world order

Extract from Tomorrow's World Order

WELCOME NOTE
Greetings!!
I personally welcome you all to this new chapter in mankind's history and to a period of enlightenment in new thinking and diverse ways never evaluated before of doing things but nevertheless a journey we must undertake as a people to reach our intended destination. I personally believe humanity has failed. Full stop! Humanity has opted for the cheaper, inferior quick ways of doing things, yet the most destructive ones rely on outdated ways of going about every aspect of life. Humanity has opted for weapons as a solution to everything. Yes, make cheaper weapons and use these to get the most expensive things unfairly and below market price. I am a businessperson as well and I understand the rationale behind this approach; make cheaper items and use these to get all the expensive ones. Makes sense. But that makes sense if this is the only option. I understand your underlying rationale, as well as, should I say, your methods of dealing with the economy, the financial aspects, the environmental or even the political methods which are outdated and honestly not fit for the purpose. Humankind has failed to think out of the box. He has opted for the quick, easy methods which are short-sighted therefore just concerned with solving short-term issues. But what if there is a clever, even better way of doing things with the only drawback being that it requires bold guts and superior thinking and relies on the foresightedness of the decision-maker? Yes, there is a solution to all global problems. The only method to take humanity to the next level. A perfect method that makes everyone better off. A method that takes humanity to levels of development and wealth never witnessed before. The only way it was intended but also one that requires brave minds and bold guts because this means changing what we have been doing for the past 2000 years. They say hard habits die hard. Your leaders in the past have opted to silence the bold and the brave rather than change their ways. But now they have no option. Time is never on their side anymore. For the past seventy years, we have seen them try all the tactics to eliminate today's problems, but I tell you this; the problems and issues at that time are still the issues now. The current system has crashed. Humankind had chance after chance to change and take the right road out of the defensive stages to

Networking and Cooperation the way it is intended but there was no overseer or leader bold enough to show them how and which path to follow. Wars were signals to humankind for him to change. Okay, your leaders tried to change soon after the World Wars and opted for peace but after the memories of the war-traumas had vanished so as the need to advance ahead and change for good. A global leader was lacking. One unbiased and not representing any nation, institution, or cult. One to put down a platform and laws that will make the transition easy. Soon after the wars, in most cases two years after witnessing the traumas of the war, the mind seemed to have forgotten and soon humankind was at it again; killing women and children using weapons and wars to get whatever he needed. Killing millions of the innocent and defenseless to 'control others for peace purposes, to lower prices of expensive resources like oil, etc. But I ask you this. What peace? Whose peace? Do you honestly believe that the innocent women and children who died and are still dying because of wars, sanctions, invasions, etc. do not want peace too? I do not bloody care what justifications they give for all this. To all humankind, peace starts with these. The women and children who are the most precious group of any society but who are sadly viewed as easy targets to be used as baits through sanctions and so on to drive political agendas, etc. I say we must put an end to all this. I understand in the past humankind had no lasting solutions for all global problems. This was his downfall, but we are saying we have produced a solution. There is a way to solve all global problems. Ignorance can never suffice, nor can it ever be relied upon. We have shown the way in this book and as such with immediate effect we have drawn a line and written our laws that everyone must obey. These laws are common; currently known as the Jus Cogens that no one can claim not to know. Everyone knows that it is wrong to kill the innocent, defenseless people of any society yet the most valuable of any society through whatever means, sanctions, invasions, poverty, etc. So, as such, we have banned all things giving your leaders 'rights to murder' these precious people of any society. Things are never going to be the same again. We anticipated resistance and have introduced new ways of dealing with evil. Trust me, there is no way out. Our laws will sink them down. Our system is fair and just. It is universal and I guarantee you today that we already have global appeal. What we stand for is what everyone; the young, old, rich, poor, no matter what background, genetic heritage standing, or sexual orientation wishes for and wants. What we stand for is everyone's dream. We stand for all humanity and will provide solutions to help every nation on earth witness riches and levels of wealth never seen before. Our plans are bold and genuine and will solve all global problems. It is a tough road, but I guarantee you wealth never witnessed before, happiness and peace of mind. I am ready. Are you ready to change the world for the better? What is not to like about banning wars through effective war-banning-laws? Banning weapons forever. Banning sanctions. Banning reliance on fossil fuels is the main trigger of all wars and needlessly deaths of women and children. It is just a fossil fuel; once it is gone, it has gone, what is not to like to start now planning the future through searching for alternate reliable, clean energy sources while saving lives of people who would otherwise end up dead due to invasions meant to beat the oil queues. At the same time, fighting climate change. All current vehicles relying on oil and other fossil fuels, to be banned by a certain date. Imagine the military instead of killing, they will be creating. Instead of destroying they will be building. Do you know that it is a crime for our best boys and girls [in soldiers] to die needlessly? Gone are the days when your leaders reduced the government's bill through sacrificing thousands and wiping off thousand names off the soldier-salary-list: sending them out there unequipped well and facing never seen before threats in roadside bombs, etc. without proper informational-intelligence. Everyone must be accountable and should recognize and obey our laws. Life shall be valued and the right to life shall mean that in every sense of the phrase. Trust me, after reading this book you will know that I mean business. This is a global movement, and you MUST be part of this New World Order.

People; join us and be part of Tomorrow's World Order [TWO]. Change is imminent and inevitable. Be on the winning side. It is a win-win situation. But first, you MUST read this book and understand what we stand for and our methods. Let today make a better tomorrow for everyone even if not for us, let it be for our children. Thank You. I am the Founder and President of Tomorrow's World Order. A global movement not biased or linked to any nation nor cult for that matter. A movement to solve all global issues through new laws, new methods and leading the way. We are Sovereign in our own right and have our own currency that will revolutionize life as we know it. An investment for you as well as you can buy our global currency that will function as the New Single Reserve Global Currency also while tackling global issues, a win-win situation. Are you ready?

JOIN US TODAY!

Tomorrow's World Order.

Your Future, Your Say. Building a Better Today.

Founder and President

Mr. David Gomadza   Signed 08/07/2019   0044771920295

The First Global President of the World
www.twofuture.world
info@twofuture.world

Conclusion

Do not expect clever aliens to come and build structures that protect us from the ever-changing climate. We are the drivers of the world and of the future and the burden is upon us to act now. To sacrifice for the entire world and future generations and put our personal interests and differences aside and work together.

I am not calling for a change in perspective regarding climatic change now. But I am saying fund the projects we are going to build. That means each country is depositing US$1 million with us so that we can use these funds to cushion against climatic change, effects of wars and all humanitarian crises. We take the bull by the horn and act fast. Some people acted fast, and we have proof of their sacrifice in the pyramids all over around the world. Imagine 4500 years ago people embarked on such projects to make sure we are here today.

Who knows, we are still here on earth as humans because of these structures.

It is a fact that pyramids or triangles protect against climatic and all atmospheric forces as such we must act fast and we want this money as soon as possible even if that means countries simply printing money to give us so be it.

Others sacrificed so that we are here today, and we are in an even better position than them.

Funding wars that kill women and children is against what we stand for.

Let us work together and protect the future generations.

This project will create jobs.

This project will introduce the need to be initiative-taking about all disasters, climatic or political ones.

We can act in advance and prevent unnecessary deaths.

Anyone against my ideas is against all humanity for I stand for humanity.

I hope everyone will jump on this journey with me and I   promise I will take you all to a new stage of development where there are no wars or harsh climatic disasters like the stage we are entering.

I am your leader and embrace change. If not, change will change you.

Signed

David Gomadza

First Global President of the World
00447719202595

www.twofuture.world
info@twofuture.world
davidgomadza@hotmail.com

ABOUT DAVID GOMADZA

I am the First Global President of the World
Visit
www.twofuture.world

www.ingramcontent.com/pod-product-compliance
Lightning Source LLC
Chambersburg PA
CBHW051401250726
48656CB00006B/2212